To Larry.

Herman is alive and WELL !!!

Jim Unger
1980

THE SECOND
HERMAN
TREASURY

Books in the Andrews and McMeel Treasury Series

Other Popular Herman Collections

THE SECOND HERMAN TREASURY

by JIM Unger

Andrews and McMeel, Inc.

A Universal Press Syndicate Company

Kansas City ● New York ● Washington

ISBN: 0-8362-1155-3 paperback
       0-8362-1156-1 cloth
Library of Congress Catalog Card Number 80-67423

Special thanks for helping me catalog these comics to my brother Steve, who chews dog biscuits, and to my brother Bob, who doesn't.

"The artist, knowing that beauty is perceived in the eye of the beholder, strives by whatever means, to broaden the perception of others in the hope that they will share his joy."

— JIM UNGER

Ever since I was a little kid, I was absolutely convinced that the world was crazy.

There I was, a defenseless child, and they had everything completely sewn up before I even got here. They had it all organized, and it was utter chaos. To make things worse, someone was dropping bombs on London, where I lived, and I hadn't even done anything!

For the first couple of years, they left me alone to watch the ducks. Things really started to get messy when I had to learn the local language. As soon as I was able to understand, they told me I had been assigned a nationality, a race, and a religion. Needless to say, they already had a name picked out for me.

I eventually realized I would have to blend in for a few years, so when I got to school I pretended everything made sense. I even learned the words to the school song.

One thing that bothered me in school was their attitude that almost anything anyone did that was organized by the school was tremendous. When I ran 299th in the school's annual cross-country race, they said it was tremendous. They said everyone was tremendous, even the girl I had beaten. The kid who came in first wasn't allowed to show how happy he must have been feeling and someone even suggested that maybe he should apologize to the rest of us. It didn't pay to be too good at anything!

In those carefree days, the "sports afternoon" was supposed to be our highlight of the week, but we had to follow the rules and be serious. Winning was of minor importance, but screaming out after being hit in the knee by a cricket ball immediately brought to question one's genealogy. Screaming wasn't cricket. I used to walk slowly off the field of play and scream behind some bushes. About that time, I had begun to suspect I was from another planet.

Lunchbreak was always the most fun thing about school. Everyone ate sandwiches during geography to avoid wasting valuable playing time during lunch. For sixty solid minutes, we played soccer with a tennis ball. We kicked, and shouted, and had a marvelous time (though the adults didn't consider it a "sport"). They used to allow us to run around like that and get all sweaty provided we wore our jackets and ties. The school was very civilized.

As soon as we were back inside the building, we used to steam up all the windows during English Literature.

"You're not getting an encyclopedia! You can walk to school like I had to."

"As soon as my arms get tired, I'll come down and you can have a go."

"Good King Wen-ces-las looked out...on the feast of Steeeephen..."

"Give me about a week's warning before they let you out of here and I'll give the kitchen the old 'once-over.'"

"You've just turned this restaurant into a 'non-profit' organization."

"Look at this! Even the garbage pail's got ulcers!"

"If I've got to tell the whole truth and nothing but the truth, what sort of fair trial is this gonna be?"

"The way we treat a headache here is to divert your attention to something else."

"Don't pull a face. Maybe the first seven horses will be disqualified."

"We can't elope. I haven't got a suitcase."

"It's the airport! Your suitcase is in Alaska and your brown bag is on the way to Singapore."

"I admit it looks horrible but it's still not grounds for divorce."

"Got any wide-bottom shirts?"

"No thank you. My husband's a reformed wino!"

"This fortune cookie says,'Very sorry, your overcoat stolen.'"

"Mommy, Herman said he'd love you to come for the weekend."

"We been married 50 years, 60 years or 70 years?"

"You can wait for him if you like. He's doing six months for 'embezzlement.'"

"That's the first time I've seen your mother leave the table without a second helping."

"You one of those 'speed-readers'?"

"Did you remember to bring my suntan oil?"

"I claim this planet in the name of Bluggrovia."

"Quit griping! D'you want your windows washed or not?"

"What's the matter with you! Can't you save that for during the commercials?"

"Take that back and cook it! It's already eaten half of the french fries."

"Is the guy in the green jacket the one who complained about the baked potatoes?"

"Boy! Did you see that ugly kid?"

"Take your time; just walk down the line and pick out the man who told you he was an 'out-of-work jockey'!"

"In describing your 'general physical appearance,' I'll just say you're looking for a girl with a good sense of humor."

"I wouldn't call it a blind date. It was more like a close encounter of the third kind."

"When you've got a minute, I'll have a box of parrot food."

"This was in the garbage compacter. It's either my hair-piece or the cat."

"Albert, if you want a sandwich, they're $10 each!"

"It's our new electronic t.v. game called 'Prize Fight.'"

"How do you plead to the charge of speeding?"

"Sorry about your window, I'm practicing for the Olympics."

"Mr. Kelly, that man's here about the job. He looks a bit drippy."

"They say you get what you pay for: It cost me
4 bucks to get married."

"You'll get used to that! A fireman lives upstairs."

"It was in the freezer—must have thawed out!"

"Number FOUR."

"Boy! I'm glad you're still awake. I was captured by a UFO and taken to another planet."

"You'd better not bring my brother anything!"

"I'm charging you a dollar for whatever it is you've got in your mouth."

"Take a seat. It'll be about two days."

"I don't know what it was, but it sure could run."

"Lights out!"

"The neck's too tight."

"He may as well have mine, now!"

"You can't buy one lettuce anymore. You
have to get a package of 10."

27

"You haven't signed these traveler's checks."

"A 300-year sentence is not so bad nowadays.
With good behavior you can be out by August."

"Waiter! There's a revolting four-letter word
in this alphabet soup."

"You been grocery shopping down at the
garbage dump again?"

"$84 for labor! Wow, what an honor! Johnny
Carson changed my plugs."

"I'm well aware it's still under warranty. So what?"

"Is this the first time he's been outside today?"

"You can rent my room and keep all the money
if you like."

"I still think I'd like a second opinion."

"What you're looking at could make you a very rich man."

"How many times have I told you not to run with the wedding cakes?"

"Why would I marry you for your money? There must be easier ways for me to get my hands on 45 bucks!"

"Thanks for doing my homework last night. The teacher thinks I'm retarded!"

2.

The first two words they teach you when you're a kid are "good" and "bad." They don't explain them fully at the time, but it becomes apparent that when you do something that meets the approval of all those around you, you're doing "good." "Bad"means something that those around you find disagreeable. This polarity has absolutely nothing whatsoever to do with right or wrong. For exactly the same deed, the same human being can either receive a shiny new medal or face a firing squad, depending upon where he, or she, gets off the bus. You have to keep your sense of humor.

You cannot explain "organized swimming," unless you accept the fact that all school kids are conditioned. Every Wednesday morning in the pouring rain, our whole class had to troop down to the local indoor pool for the weekly torture. They were so programmed, they used to start shouting and whooping it up as soon as they got inside the lockers. Everyone else could change into his trunks and be in the ice in eighteen seconds. Balancing on one foot on a soaking wet tiled floor, shivering uncontrollably, it would take me almost the whole hour to get undressed. I guess I knew what was coming.

No one expects to get two pints of water up his nose when he gingerly lowers himself down the pool steps at the shallow end. But I always did! Gulping down mouthfuls of the stuff, it occurred to me that this same liquid had been providing cool comfort to 5000 pairs of feet over the past few weeks. The others were oblivious.

Everyone had to take music lessons once a week, and some of the more glassy-eyed students pretended to like playing the violin. Even worse, some of them said they liked listening to it. So I tried it. But after five years of violin lessons, I was thrown out for not being serious enough. Four hours of practice completely wasted!

"Try to think of something for me to invent."

"Did I say we had to plant them 4 feet deep? I meant 4 inches."

"They're wearing them like that these days."

"I don't know how you can stay up all night and watch horror movies."

"Anyone here fly a 747?"

"Grandpa's bought an Afro wig."

"Can I make a phone call before I commit myself?"

"Do you recognize this pan as the one your wife used?"

"You sure you couldn't find any larger nails?"

"The jury has found you not guilty, but I'm going to give you 2 years just to be on the safe side."

"You're absolutely right, I'm at the wrong house."

"Are you wearing furry socks?"

"You're lucky you were wearing your seatbelt."

"You've laid the new rug!"

"I put the candles on the cake like you said, and the box caught fire."

"I didn't see that. Did you get him with blueberry or pecan?"

"I don't know if they told you outside but I never employ anyone over 5 feet tall."

"I don't care what I look like, I'm not getting mutilated by hair-rollers."

"I thought I'd make them long to keep your knees warm."

"I told you it wouldn't stay up there."

"I told her, the day I do the dishes is the day the sky falls in."

"Surely you can appreciate we need a height regulation in the police force?"

"What's the big idea sticking this on the back wall of the garage?"

"Your aunt Frieda has left you $50,000 if you'll promise to look after her cat."

"Sorry I'm late. I got caught in traffic."

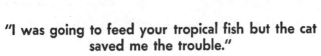
"I was going to feed your tropical fish but the cat saved me the trouble."

"It's not gonna kill you to help me with the dishes once in a while."

"Are you taking your bikini?"

"Don't forget the syrup."

44

"You can't rush my chunky stew."

"Have you been out of the country more than 24 hours?"

"Can I change channels?"

"Your dinner's getting cold."

"If this is gonna make me strong and handsome, I think you'd better eat it."

"Doc, can you give me something to make me feel a bit more energetic?"

"What's wrong with me picking up a few extra bucks on the way to the movies?"

"And another thing. Because he has to be at work by 5 a.m., I get stuck with all the breakfast dishes."

"I hate giving these injections. Look at my hands shaking."

"I told you not to jump around upstairs. Look at my lamp!"

"Hey Bud, I need change. Give me two twenties for this five."

"How much longer you gonna be in here? The bread ran out last week and now the coffee and butter are gone."

"I've lost the use of my legs!"

"Mother's sent you a book for your birthday. She says, 'Tell him it's got lots of pictures.'"

"Wake up. I heard a crash!"

"Well look at that! The store across the street has the same binoculars for $15 less."

"I can't understand it! He just burst in and shot my violin."

"Silly old me! I've been superintendent of this apartment building for 25 years and I thought I'd seen everything."

"All the girls are off sick!"

"You're what we call 'a reverse rejection case.' I've got to find a suitable kidney that won't reject YOU."

"Go ahead! I'll only bleed all over your new rug."

"D'you believe this! It said, 'Umbrellas 50% Off.'"

"I told you not to try to adjust it yourself."

"OK! As it's our 25th anniversary, I'll make the coffee. Where d'you get the water from?"

"Your hat's full of cigarette butts again!"

"I'm sure you three will be pleased to hear I'm agreeing to your 15% pay demand. 5% each!"

"I think you'll find, Sir, our brochure says 'safe beach.' You must have gone into the water."

"Is it too spicy?"

"I'm going soon! Your house is always drafty."

"We've lost your stuff, but you get first choice of any bag off Flight 601 from Athens."

"WILL YOU KEEP YOUR ARMS DOWN!"

"Can't he go and watch some violence on TV?"

"Put me out of my misery! Which one of you types 140 words per minute?"

"As a last resort, this final attachment will slide into the customer's pocket and suck out $160."

"The only lead we've got on the guy who grabbed your wallet and ran off is that he's probably an Olympic gold medalist."

"See, I got an 'A' in 'Disco Appreciation.'"

"Why do I get the feeling that if I drop this check it'll jump up and break the window?"

"You'll love this place. Palm trees, sandy beaches and a restaurant every 30 feet."

"It's my old flashlight. I couldn't get any candles."

"Oh, good! Is that my other knitting needle?"

"D'you get a lot of rain on your planet?"

"What are you here for?"

3.

Eventually, the time comes when every teenager has to face the trauma of leaving school. My entire family, including rich aunts and uncles, had just enough money between them to buy a toaster. So I knew a university was out of the question, but I just couldn't face the idea of getting a job.

Going to a strange new place every day to work with strange, serious people, filled me with horror. I remember one faint glimmer of interest, when somebody mentioned "getting paid," but all I really wanted to do was to go home and go to bed until the fuss died down.

All those years of straight A's and impressing the teachers, and they were throwing me out into the world!

In those final dark days, we were counseled by a career advisor. He had a darn in his sweater, rode a rusty old bicycle to school every day, and knew everything there was to know about getting a good, well-paid job. He sat at the front of the class and smiled knowingly as each spotty sixteen-year-old decided then and there to devote the rest of his working life to being an accountant or a bank clerk. One case of acne drew a visible sneer when he mumbled something about becoming a sign-painter because his father was a sign-painter. What a waste of violin lessons!

When your name begins with a "U," you're nearly always last to do everything. Wheeler and Wilson had their own problems. Anyway, my turn to be the focus of attention with the career advisor finally came, and I told him I wanted to be a swimming instructor in a nudist colony. They loved it! I was such a character. The career advisor said that since I found the proceedings so comical, I would probably end up in insurance.

Two weeks later, I did.

"Happy birthday, boss. All the guys got together
and bought you a new padlock for your wallet."

"Grandma, you didn't borrow my sweater,
did you?"

"Great checkup! Have some candy."

"The important thing right now is that he
wants to get out of lion taming."

62

"At these prices, I've got about 20 seconds to recover and get out the main gate."

"Anyone know where I can find the gift shop?"

"You go and have your family reunion and I'll meet you by the penguins."

"Can't you sit down! This is supposed to be a picnic."

"You should hear what she just called him!"

"Feeling any better after a hot bath?"

"It's a real treat to talk to someone who doesn't keep laughing."

"I told you not to keep asking me to dance."

"He doesn't have an account with us."

"Hey, boss! This cute little fella wants to know why we're three years behind with the car payment."

"Your account is $28 overdrawn."

"You better make sure I get it back Friday."

"So you left school in 1937 and became a bank robber. What happened after that?"

"I know you're a veterinarian. Regular doctors won't touch him!"

"Folks, the main reason you're not getting a good picture is because you bought yourselves a microwave oven."

"You're the one who wanted to get married. You're the one who wanted kids. You wanted the house and the furniture and now YOU want to be LIBERATED!"

"Is there a reverse switch on the drill?"

"Don't make a face; it's cheaper than food."

"They got me for $28 tax last week. How did you make out?"

"I never enjoy a comedy with you laughing all the way through it."

"This one's called 'Here Comes the Sun.'"

"Your mother left her teeth in our bathroom.
They're just starting to slow down!"

"As it's your first jump, we'll see if we can find
you a better parachute."

"Your father lost a dollar here in 1968."

"She came straight out of 'Jams and Jellies'
without signaling."

"Can't you answer the front door bell while I'm cooking?"

"I'll pay for them and we'll call it your birthday present."

"I just can't believe I'm gonna look like you when I'm 35."

"That must be one nervous parrot!"

"I'm not worried. If I'm not smart enough to get a good job, I can always teach."

"Don't get any of that stuff on your father."

"I spell relief d-i-v-o-r-c-e."

"I just figured out why they call you 'The Mouse.'"

"Sorry about the two scars. We had your X-ray upside down."

"This is ridiculous! I raise you a nickel and you throw in four aces."

"We can't complain. It's their wedding anniversary."

"They're all out, but I'll tell them you called."

"If it doesn't itch, don't worry about it."

"I bet they try to keep our $5 deposit!"

"There's nothing wrong with him. He just does that to make me look stupid."

"You got a Superman T-shirt for him—32-inch chest?"

"I'm 65 today! I guess I'm retired."

"Take a look in here! Five bags of mail, two sets of encyclopedias and a brand-new vacuum cleaner."

"How do you feel about me going to my sister's for two weeks?"

"Take that thing off or I'll fine you for contempt."

"Mix me up another four quarts of this coffee. I think I'll try it in my transmission."

"Got any more shaving cream?"

"I've gotta have identification. You must have some sort of pilot's license?"

"Have you got a smoke alarm I can switch off while I'm cooking?"

"Does he bite?"

"You've eaten all the nuts!"

"GET THAT THING OFF MY COFFEE TABLE!"

"Excuse me for being born."

"Where d'yer keep the bubblegum?"

"You do realize I'm going to have to report this, Thompson?"

"Don't eat it if your gums are sore."

"I wish you wouldn't keep sitting so close to my cactus."

"'A little dessert,' not 'a little desert.'"

"This is the guy who was stung by a bee."

I had to borrow my father's best suit and be "interviewed." For a whole hour, the manager at the insurance company explained the merits of the pension plan, which in my case was due sometime after the year 2000. After that, I was conducted on a brief tour of the premises to pin-point my very own desk and chair, and the men's room. I don't think I was suppose to go anywhere else.

I think the manager could see I wasn't too thrilled about spending the next forty-eight years at that desk. He kept telling me I'd soon get used to it. To add insult to injury, the place was an hour's train-ride away! While I still had my father's suit on, I went over to the public library and looked up the word "migraine." Someone said it was going around.

My first day at work was awful. I was required to wear a three-piece suit and a collar and tie. It was like being at a wedding for nine hours. After the first ten minutes, I was sure I was going to pass out; but insurance is very civilized and a trainee filing clerk without a jacket is unthinkable.

Returning home, I was totally exhausted. In one day, I had earned enough money to pay my train fare for the whole week. When I realized that it would be another two weeks before I got the hard cash, I didn't feel too bad about not actually having done anything.

They didn't pay too much attention to me on the second day. They even gave me something to do. I soon realized that jokes weren't allowed and conversation was kept to a minimum, even when the manager's door was closed. I found out later he had the place bugged. I correctly filed nine yellow cards, so they said I could be in charge of the letter-stamping machine. I couldn't wait to get home and tell my parents!

On the third day, my ulcer started. I had only forty-seven years, fifty-one weeks, and three days to go for the pension, and the alarm clock didn't go off. Even Hermans know they can't be late on their third day. When I woke up, I had exactly seven minutes to catch the Insurance Express. I saved precious time by washing and shaving all the way down High Street and hopped up three flights of railway steps, on either leg, tying my shoe laces. The train was twenty minutes late but I still steamed up all the windows. I had coated teeth all day.

"You did very well on our IQ test!"

"I hope you're not walking across my clean floor."

"Grandpa gave me his transistor radio."

"What would the 'widow's benefits' be, say, six months from now?"

"Repeat after me: 'Hypnotherapy is worth $60 an hour.'"

"Phone the newspaper; I just found a second piece of pork in this can of beans!"

"Is that chicken too well cooked for you?"

"You won't be able to paint the ceiling like that."

"Put those back!"

"Got a table for two near the exit?"

"If you want instant coffee, you'll have to wait!"

"He won't eat!"

"I'm making her a coat the same as yours."

"Here's that book you ordered, 'Income Tax Made Easy.'"

"I told you to sip it."

"That car you sold me is only getting about six miles to a gallon of gas."

"I told you you'd need more than a gallon."

"We're having a party downstairs. D'you wanna come?"

"Did you remember to send your mother a birthday card?"

"Dig up your father or you won't get any ice cream."

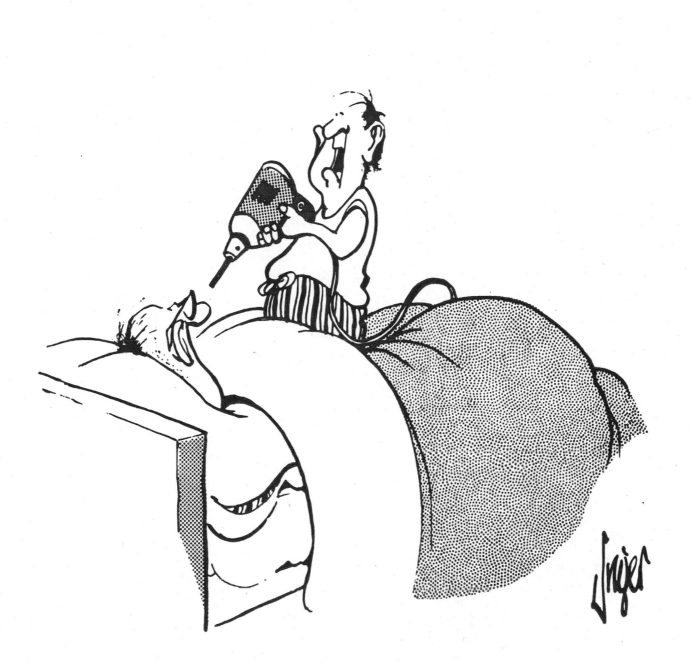

"I'm NOT going to the dentist."

"Your wife's got a very bad case of sunburn on her tongue."

"I get a real sharp pain when I do this."

"He's lost his worm again."

"Any diet drinks?"

"I could have sworn you were related to Sophia Loren."

"We've got to leave in four hours. Here's your lipstick!"

"I won't have a table for 20 minutes. Here's your soup."

"You left that back door open again."

"Why didn't you say you wanted them both the same size?"

"First time I've seen gold-plated tools."

"Dad, the cat got married!"

"Would I be correct in assuming you don't have experience as a plastic surgeon?"

"If the house was on fire, who would you save first, me or the cat?"

"Gimme the keys to your company car!"

"We forgot the food!"

"I'd say you picked a bad time to fire your cook."

"Are they playing overtime? You must be absolutely exhausted."

"Is this the guy who's been charged with impersonating a police officer?"

"Your sister's had another kid."

"All our 'extra large' jeans are 34-inch waist."

"The management has gone on strike demanding we take a 10 percent pay cut."

"What does he want to eat, a bowl of ants?"

"What have you been feeding that parrot?"

"Look at your best shirt."

"How much do you want for these brown ones?"

"Mirror, mirror, on the wall, who's the fair......"

"You've got seven new fillings on the left side."

PASSENGERS WITHOUT TICKETS

"I think he's saying he wants a one-way ticket to Egypt."

"HARRY...HOW MUCH ARE THESE LAXATIVE PILLS?"

"Are you comfortable down there, Daddy?"

"You can't be putting on weight already! You only quit smoking 20 minutes ago."

"Why are you such a messy eater?"

"Dobson, I've just figured out a way for you personally to save this company $750 a month."

"He can't get used to your new hairpiece."

"Did you mean be home by 10 o'clock tonight or
10 o'clock tomorrow morning?"

"I told you not to marry her."

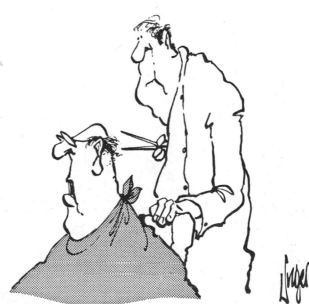

"Just trim the sides and the back."

"Are you a good runner?"

"A guy tipped me 20 bucks once!"

"That's 10 rings. Shall we try for 11?"

"Here's a guy who puts his mouth where his money is."

"Is he allowed a plea of insanity for a parking ticket?"

"If he can't talk how do you know his name is Ralph?"

"The basement's full of soapy water."

"I'd tell your father, but he probably lent you the hat."

"You should never try to fix an electric shaver."

"Nature is a great compensator. You're probably a super mountain climber."

"How many times have I told you not to snap your fingers while I'm extracting teeth under hypnosis?"

"It's hardly sex discrimination just because I can't picture you as a topless waitress."

5.

The months at the insurance company dragged on. I was up to fifty yellow cards a day. Although most of my old school chums had been promoted to presidents or directors of their respective companies, we remained good friends. We often went out together, and as I was moonlighting on the weekends, delivering laundry, I didn't mind lending them money.

About that time, my friends and I started to get really serious about girls. When you're serious about girls, you're not a filing clerk, you're an airline pilot! I had to learn a whole new set of rules. Although we pretended we had, none of us had any experience with the opposite sex. When I was eleven, I used to practice a few surgery techniques on my sister's best friend, Pamela, but that didn't count because neither of us knew what we were doing. We used to take turns being the patient. Neither of us understood why we felt so "medical." She had a talk with her mother one afternoon, and I didn't see much of her after that.

None of the insurance guys showed any interest in girls. The more civilized you were, the less you showed you liked girls. Truck drivers appreciated girls, but lawyers didn't. Construction workers whistled at them, and insurance guys pretended they didn't see them. I knew, sooner or later, I would have to choose between my precious pension and driving a truck for a construction company. It was all very confusing.

My first real date was with a girl who worked the switchboard at one of our branch offices. I never actually saw her in the flesh, so to speak, but I spoke to her on the telephone from time to time. I promised myself I would be really cool, but as the fateful day drew near, I had already picked out names for our kids. I was so excited, I blew three months pay on a new pair of leather shoes and had to squeak all the way to the town hall, hoping no one would notice the flowers stuffed in the back of my jacket. I got so nervous after waiting six and a half hours, I was beginning to hope she wouldn't show up.

It was only two in the morning, but I finally decided to accept the obvious and walked over to Pamela's house, thinking she may like the flowers. When I got there, all the lights were out. I threw stones at her bedroom window, but she didn't wake up. Either that, or she heard the squeaking coming up the road and knew it was me.

I never liked the taste of beer, however everyone else seemed to love the stuff, and I didn't want to be left out of anything. I was assured it would "grow on me."

One night, we all went out to a bar. I was the only novice drinker in the party, so I decided to limit my intake. After drinking about fourteen pints, I realized I'd set my limit too high. I had to be carried out. I think I spent the rest of the evening, face down on someone's bathroom floor, counting the tiles. It was all part of growing up. I had a headache for three months.

"No don't switch it on; just explain the advantages
over other insect repellents."

"We've got the same grandchildren! Are you
my first husband Harold?"

"How's he feeling? I badly need a pair
of kidneys."

"Will you turn that fan down!"

"It's the barman's little joke. First drink's on the house."

"Don't tell me what it is until I've eaten it."

"I had to shorten the pants quite a lot."

"It's your own fault for forgetting the can of cat food."

"If you have to sneeze, do it during
the lunchbreak."

"That stove should be in a war museum."

"Your green pills are all gone. Do you wanna
take a blue and a yellow?"

"This place hasn't been a Japanese restaurant for
over two years."

"He gets uncomfortable meeting strangers."

"Apart from your neck, how are you
feeling generally?"

"200 miles to the gallon!"

"It's come to my attention that you own five cars
and an ocean-going yacht."

"Sandra, bring me a paper towel."

"Forget about me meeting the willowy blonde! I just need the name of one horse."

"Don't blame the cat. What would you do if someone sat on you?"

"Why can't I have the movie on and you watch the game during the commercials?"

"The recipe says a pinch of spice. I thought it said a 'pound.'"

"You here again?"

"It's still raining."

"Watch out for that loose stair!"

"He's glued his feet again."

"What do you mean, 'Where's the car?'
This is the car."

"That should clear the rug."

"What have you done to your hair?"

"What are all these doing in the trunk of the car?"

"Was the subway faster than taking the car?"

"Watch this! It'll go in two bites."

"What are you hiding behind your back?"

"Shhhhhhhhhh."

"I suppose I'll be a male chauvinist pig if I ask you to be on time tomorrow morning."

"I just bought this package of batteries and it says, 'Batteries not included.' "

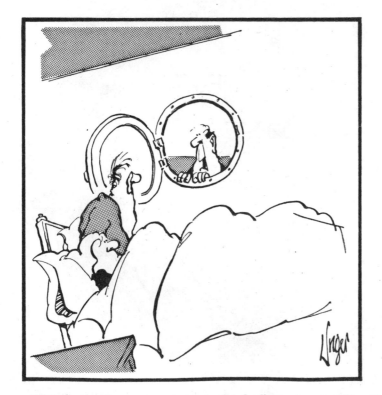

"This is my first cruise. What's the bell ringing for?"

"Nice to meet you at last. You must be 'Linebacker.' "

"You must be crazy, driving 800 miles in one day."

"Dr. Burns says you need two more appointments."

"I've got some matches somewhere."

"Mr. Soames here is the best teacher we have."

"Don't forget, Buster. If it wasn't for me and Frankie you'd be paying a lot more income tax."

"Is the lady coming back, sir?"

"You've been practicing for an hour and you've only hit it once."

"You here again, Carole!"

"I wish you'd wear a hat in there. I've been looking all over for you."

"I'm really proud of you! This time tomorrow, you'll have been on your diet a whole week."

"You must have got it wet!"

"If you want to see something 'real cheap,' take a look in the mirror."

"What do you mean, the lesson's over? I've got another 20 minutes."

"Never shout at your plumber."

"You're a lot uglier than your pictures."

"He put our clock-radio in his sack!"

"It must be pretty good wine for $6 a bottle."

"You can put your left down now."

"Dad put glue in her denture cleaner."

"What are the chances of exchanging a red and green
shirt with blue stripes?"

"That was lucky!"

"This new night fragrance is called 'Surrender.'"

"I've completely lost track. Is it ONE million B.C. or TWO million B.C.?"

"Would you say you are, 'extremely happy,' 'happy,' 'average' or 'bored stiff'?"

"Can you eat turkey leftovers again?"

"Who do you think's gonna drink that?"

6.

When I was eighteen, I had to do two years in the army. There wasn't a war on at the time, but I was pretty sure someone would start something within twenty-four months. I thought it would make a nice change from insurance.

Not everyone had to do military service. Girls and college students were excluded, along with anyone bright enough to fail the medical or intelligent enough to be declared unstable. Out of all of England, that left about five hundred of us. Of those five hundred, half were too sick to care about doing two years in the army. I was in the second half.

I couldn't wait to get my macho uniform and laze around under the palm trees on some tropical island. I wasn't stupid. I'd seen all the posters.

After a two-hour train ride, clutching a bottle of suntan lotion, I was picked up at a remote railway station and driven to the camp in the back of an open truck. It was raining like mad. I must have been looking at the wrong posters because the camp turned out to be a cluster of wooden huts in the middle of a field. The nearest town was eighteen miles away, and there was one bus a day.

I think I spent almost the entire two years there.

"He's the equivalent of 49 years old, but he's not intelligent enough to get crabby!"

"You the guy with the chain-saw for sale?"

"Congratulations, Mrs. Parker."

"Someone's stolen my bicycle!"

"I always knew there was something different about you, Charlie."

"Boy, that takes me back! I haven't seen a suit like that for 30 years."

"There's a 200-foot monster outside and he tells her to bolt the door."

"Please have your tickets ready."

"Get down. I'm knitting this stuff for the girl next door."

"Here's your pizza! We ran out of boxes."

"Hey! Do you wanna see a U.F.O.?"

"One day you'll realize that the people capable of running the country are too smart to get into politics."

"So it looks like a nice day tomorrow."

"Your mother went jogging and got a ticket for 'malicious damage' to the sidewalk."

"The police towed away the car, so I bought another one."

"It's not my fault we're short of beds."

"They won't come near me since I gave them some of my wife's homemade cake."

"Left home without your money, did you?"

"Can you see anything?"

"I'm double-parked outside the courthouse."

"Oh, no, split-ends!"

"What does the Guinness Book of Records say about dishing out long sentences?"

"Sorry, I thought you were someone else."

"Look at this birth certificate—it's parchment."

"You're not gonna believe it-there's an elephant coming."

"Drop it!"

"Did you mean for it to go in the lake?"

"If you miss a payment, I press this button
and the unit self-destructs."

"You always said you liked fish."

"He's not walking backwards; you've got the leash on the wrong end!"

"Take my advice: Get yourself a good strong woman and don't worry about looks!"

"How much do I owe you so far?"

"Why don't I recommend a plastic surgeon to do something about that nose?"

"Got a room with a balcony?"

"From your X-ray, I'd say you eat too fast."

"I'm sorry! I guess I didn't see the sign."

"If gasoline were $5 a gallon, do you realize how many camels we could sell in Los Angeles."

"Mr. and Mrs. Roberts to see you, Doctor."

"If I find out you're faking, there'll be no 'yummies' for a week."

"Maybe I'd better get going soon."

"They say behind every successful man there's a woman. Here's a picture of my wife."

"He's here now! Seal off the building."

"It wasn't three somersaults. It was two and a half!"

"Take your time. The plane doesn't leave for 3 minutes."

"Eat up! There's no sense getting a load of dishes dirty."

"If you're gonna complain, you can cut it yourself."

"Don't stand too close; you'll make them homesick!"

"I know the runny green stuff is potato. What's the black gravel?"

"Has that one got blue eyes?"

"Is this too skimpy for the beach?"

"There are two bedrooms on this floor."

"Got any discarded clothing?"

"I think you're jumping to conclusions. A lot of people love carrots."

"Did you tell him 'Babylon' was a race-horse who liked to run on the outside?"

"If it's convenient, sir, I'll be on strike from 2
till 4 p.m. for a pay raise."

"Is it the meatloaf again?"

"Don't ask questions. Just see if my umbrella's
under the sink."

"Oh boy! A whole dollar. I hope it doesn't spoil me."

"Surely you must know if you have
health insurance..."

"You're supposed to rub it on your head,
not drink it!"

"In some parts of the world, whole villages
could live on your food intake."

"There's an elephant on TV and she's throwing
peanuts at it!"

"Say 'cheese.'"

"Don't you ever rinse my shirts when you wash them?"

"Don't be a grouch. He's been waiting all day for you to smoke that."

"Now snore."

"Small, medium or large?
Or need I ask?"

"She couldn't change a $20 bill."

"The computer is demanding a
complete service overhaul every six
months and two weeks off in August."

"Never missed a beat!"

"How come my photo's got all these little holes in it?"

7.

I like television better than the movies because you don't have to go out and line up to watch it. I hate lining up for anything. It's an unnatural act! But if you go anywhere, and you don't have to line up, you can be pretty sure it's not worth going.

The last time I went to the movies, I had to line up for an hour—fifty minutes before the show started and ten minutes after. After a brief discussion with the cashier about having to pay the full price of admission, I had to stagger around in total darkness among empty popcorn boxes and locate a seat behind anyone under six feet tall who was not wearing a top hat. I spent another ten minutes peeling someone's bubblegum off my sleeve, while behind me a gorilla and his wife started divorce proceedings over what constituted the difference between a "large size" and a "small size" soft drink.

I think a lot of people like opera because it's cleaner.

If I'm not busy, I'll sometimes switch off the television and go to a party. Parties are either good or bad. Bad parties usually take place under 600-watt bulbs and there are plastic covers on the upholstered furniture. If you can't fake a migraine, it's best to sit quietly and do what everyone else is doing — talk to the person you came with. The ordeal doesn't last long. Usually at around ten o'clock, someone mutters something about "beauty sleep" and everyone gets up to leave. It's always been a source of amusement for me that people with nothing to say for three hours will suddenly become excessively friendly when they know that within thirty seconds, they'll be out of your life forever. The guy who needed the beauty sleep is often the last one out.

I wish I could find out why my insides always make weird noises at dinner parties. I think I have a mental block about eating someone else's food. It could be the after-effects of the war. It doesn't matter how friendly the people are; I never have an appetite until I'm back outside in the cool night air. Then I'm starving. More often than not, I'll drive to an all-night café and think about all the delicious food I've left behind, while I'm relishing a greasy bacon sandwich washed down with gray coffee.

"Look at the bottle of perfume he bought me for my birthday!"

"It says: 'Due to rising costs, all wishes are now 50 cents.'"

"I still say we should tunnel."

"Nothing your mother does surprises me anymore."

"Feeling better? I made you a spaghetti sandwich."

"I couldn't find anything wrong with you, but you're entitled to a second opinion."

"I gotta get new glasses! I thought that was a big duck."

"I really appreciate the visit, Ralph, but you're sitting on my broken leg."

"I found your birth certificate in the attic. You're not 54, you're 91."

"What are you, a wise guy?"

"I think you need a smaller size."

"You can't be 'half-and-half.' You're either 'guilty' or 'not guilty.'"

"Don't forget to put his watch ahead two hours. We forgot that last time."

"D'you mind showing me what you have in this pocket?"

"Hey Bill, Bill!"

"I don't think you're supposed to eat the little umbrella."

"Got any spare fuses?"

"Don't you people ever feed these animals?"

"Read it yourself! It says, 'Dozen eggs, bread, milk, chocolate chip cookies.'"

"One-two-three-THROW, four-five-six-DUCK."

"Where's your fork?"

"I know you; your wife put you up to this!"

"I know you wanted a packet of fish sticks! This is all they had."

"First you buy me a new coat and now a trip to Lion Safari Park. What's got into you lately?"

"I haven't forgotten what you said to me last month."

"D'you want a wake-up call, sir?"

"Must you watch television when my sister's here?"

"Have you seen a pair of brown gloves?"

"How are you gonna get to work when it's not windy?"

"We had a tough time getting that stain out."

"You're taking a chance, wearing that dress in this neighborhood."

"I thought I told you to take your jacket off."

"Harry, quick, get over here."

"PUT THAT BACK."

"The kitchen's on fire again."

"You're not supposed to THROW it!"

"Can you identify the man who punched you in the knee?"

172

"Don't tell me I'm getting HIM."

"He's put gravy in his water pistol."

"At least she's trying to communicate."

"That guy gave us three ice-cream cones for Dad's camera."

"By the time we get in there,
all the monkeys will be worn out!"

"My mother mustn't know! I told her
you'd run off with your secretary."

"One small step for women's lib,
one giant leap toward divorce."

"Every time you press that buzzer,
just remember that I'm the one
who'll be taking out your stitches."

"Wake up. The cat's got your teeth."

"CUCKOO."

"What do you do in your spare time?"

"It's my new invention. Talk to your mother for an hour on this and it will heat the whole house for a month!"

"Dad, lend me $5,000 and I promise I'll clean my room for a whole week."

"I don't know what you're eating,
but you gave the dog a can
of spaghetti sauce!"

"What did you do to Dad's chair?"

"I see you bought a new dog."

"Where have you been? You're last!"

178

"I hear you have a room to rent."

"If you fall off your horse,
run like mad."

"I wish you wouldn't eat cookies
in bed."

"Keep your eyes open.
Two prisoners are missing!"

"Get back! You're not leaving this house with my credit cards."

"He will!"

"Your boss said you can have your job back when you get out if you tell him where the $50,000 is."

"D'you want the movie, or shall we watch the news and have a good laugh?"

180

"A bee won't sting you if
you leave it alone."

8.

"Tis no shame to have been foolish; the shame lies in not having cut the folly short." — HORACE

As soon as I realized I could never be a human, I was a lot happier. I began working for myself. Apart from all the bother of going somewhere every morning and coming home again every evening, when I was working for someone else I never had time to think. I always felt guilty if I wasn't busy "doing something." Sometimes I used to try to think by staring at a blank wall, but all I could think about was that someone would walk in and catch me thinking. So I never thought of anything.

Now I really enjoy drawing Herman. I particularly enjoy all the wonderful people I've been meeting all over North America and all the letters I receive. I am still trying to understand where Herman comes from. Everything in my life up to now has been incredibly normal, and apart from my brother chewing dog biscuits to make his teeth whiter, nothing particularly funny has happened.

Love to all.

"You got down there to do sit-ups
and fell asleep."

"The rabbits are eating all his carrots."

"I don't suppose you've got a bottle
of Thousand Island salad dressing
in your pocket, do you?"

"You weighed 100 pounds on our
wedding day, so I'm not even married
to three-quarters of you!"

"I had to give your sausages a shot with the fire extinguisher. Do you still want to eat them?"

"The soup of the day has gone off. How about the soup of tomorrow?"

"I'll give you my car and stereo if we call it off."

"I don't know why I bother cooking for you!"

"I've only got 5 cents. I'll have one big bite of this."

"Can you change $400 worth of quarters?"

"Keep it up! He's getting overconfident."

"Got change for a quarter so I can leave this guy a tip?"

"Come down here. You've ruined my plant."

"It's on sale this week for $15,000."

"Which finger is it?"

"You see, son, the grass isn't always greener on the other side of the fence."

"This book you sold me, 'There's One Born Every Minute' — it's just blank pages!"

"Sorry about your eye. Did you see where the ball went?"

"What do you think? Do I look better in the wider horns?"

"He really likes you!"

"BIGFOOT!"

"You got a dog?"

"That's the last pair I have in those!"

"It's not mashed potatoes. The french fries fell on the floor."

"This one's called, 'Bowl of Fruit on Very High Table.'"

"Do you think I should let my hair grow longer?"

"Snarl."

"Blackie!"

"You look a lot better!"

"Buzz off! You're not getting any."

"Gotcha!"

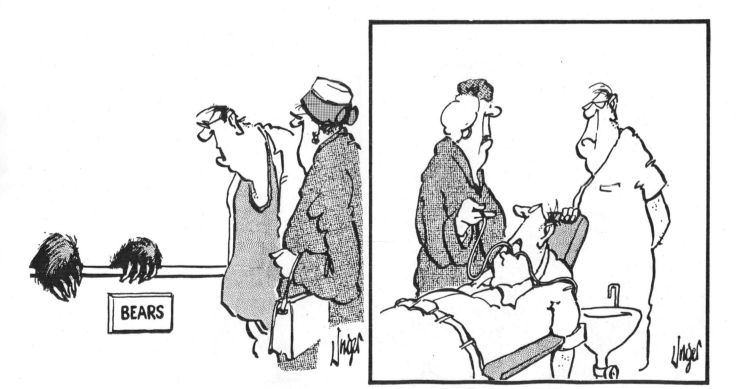

"I think he's gonna make it. Let's go!"

"He'll be OK for an hour. Let's go to lunch."

"I guessed you weren't from around here."

"D'you think they'll settle out of court for a thousand if I sue for maybe 5 million?"

"I've been looking for that!"

"Relax, I've got to test your stomach muscles."

"Throw them farther!"

"I know how you feel!
I missed a 2-inch putt once."

"Grandpa, I can't remember
which one is yours."

"What was all that
screaming outside?"

"I'm not keen on this big sponge.
All the bathwater's gone!"

"Your birthday's next week.
D'you want a surprise party?"

"It's my ex-boyfriend."

"Have you decided?"

"Have you seen my pantyhose
anywhere?"

"Nurse, run outside and
get his shoe."

"That's our pen!"

"He watched a heart transplant on
TV three days ago, and he's
still recovering."

"What do I have to do to get
some service around here?"

"Do you mind keeping
the noise down!"

"I don't care if we have been married
15 years, I'm not buying
any brushes."

"It's stopped! But I think it'll
start up again."

"Can you account for your
whereabouts in January 1907?"

"You get the parking meter and I'll buy the coffee."

"I just moved in next door. Where do you keep your lawn mower?"

"He'll be back soon. He's gone for a cherry split."

"Wake up, Dad."

"I'd better go now, Snookums.
I'm with a patient."

"Your shoes are marking the rug!"

"Coffee to go."

"I told you not to wear
that dumb hat."

"The top came off."

"You left your wallet
at the fish shop!"

"Will you buzz off!"

"This shouldn't take too long!"

"Twelve glasses of milk and 12 cookies."

"I love doing that!"

"I never have any luck with living things."

"Charlie, can you fix four flat tires?"

"Don't let them see the frying pan!"